More Praise for Psychotic Kisses

"Psychotic Kisses mixes the dark and the sensual in a way that captures the music of madness and the haze of drug-fogged lust with quick lines of quirky poetry. Darkly surreal, at times almost dadaist in execution, Steve Baba's work hits the reader like a strange dream of Bukowski. It delivers lines with all the grace of a shovel full of street-grit, but pulls no punches. This is honest poetry. This is analog expression. This is what the world looks like when we skin our eyes and dare to peer beyond the clean curves and shining lights of our digital, computer-driven sanctuaries."

E.S. Wynn, author of over 50 books and Chief Editor of Thunderune Publishing

"There are ghosts in this collection. Ghosts of living room demons and ghosts of pimple faced saints. Ghosts of heroin needles and diner-booth flashers. Steve Baba is a dutiful medium, writing down their broken worlds like he writes his own dreams and nightmares. Colors and sounds and tastes and warnings become one as we slip from poem to poem, scene to scene, along with the ghosts that inhabit them. They speak to you in fragments but they speak to you in unison. You won't get it right away, won't know what it is they're saying—until it hits you on the train/car/plane ride to home or to nowhere that what the ghosts of Psychotic Kisses were singing was a love-song for life."

Mike Joyce, Editor-in-Chief, Literary Orphans Journal

"Steve Baba's Psychotic Kisses is a surprisingly calm collection at first glance, but raw humanity, loneliness, sex, and desire roil under the surface. This collection is worth reading in the same way it's worth having a drink with a good friend after a long week."

Lindsey Lewis Smithson, Editor, Straight Forward Poetry

"Poet Steve Baba holds us in a ceremonial blaze that scorches sandstone thoughts into fiery diamonds of dazzling brilliance! A significant collection of interlaced poetic works that will remain wedded to your subconscious until death do you part..."

Jennifer Fish, poet included in the poetry anthologies The Universe Inside and Stars in Our Hearts.

Psychotic Kisses Poems

Steve Baba

Crimson Milk Press
San Francisco

Cover design by Jason Blair

Ways to contact the author:
www.stevebaba.com
facebook.com/stevebaba
twitter.com/stevenhbaba

First printing, March 2014
Printed in the USA

ISBN:0615968147
ISBN-13:9780615968148

Table Of Contents

I.

II.

III.

IV.

This time around, I am going to have a lengthy acknowledgements page. Thank you Mom and Dad for hanging with me when I was at my darkest hour. Thank you to my sisters, Andrea and Erin, whom have been supportive and loving. To my nephews Darrien, Jordan and Diego. You make uncle proud! To Jim Pacelli, who is the best friend any person could have. To Ilan Kaim, I feel like we have been life-long friends and I am glad we are such a good team. Thanks to Mark Kendra. Though we only see each other rarely, talking on the phone about life and writing is refreshing, and you are also a great friend. And A Big Thank You to Tiffany Silverman, my forever muse. I have thought of you every day since the last time we saw each other. You are the fire in my heart, the joy in my eyes, the itch in my brain. Never change.

For Malia, my niece. She is a light in a dark place for me and a welcome sight when things get tough.

I.

But It Is Scary

wolves and eggs
wolves and eggs

the tapestry was happy
but i was not

she touched the golden light
i saw the shadows as usual

dirty feet
clumps of grass
clung to the soles

i wanted to know
what the deal was

are you soft?
are you distant?

if the sun were a stone
it was a heavy one

making my face black
making the plants wither

how much can a soda can hold?
sip spit sip spit

Wary Of Life

my stomach is not
agreeing with my mind

some say it's because
i have this hunger inside
that won't go away

a choppy sea
swirling cream
i have a callous on my heart

she rubbed her forehead
trying to get rid of the wrinkles
but they were there permanently

the songs are the same
as they usually are about
this time of night

like a feather touching a finger
like a dog sleeping in the sunlight

but would it be rational
if my stomach expelled acid
into my throat?

bladder bladder
empty me now!

Greatness Is Not Good

kinky doughnuts
the squirrel chases
nuts into dark holes

don't fall
please don't fall

her masturbation techniques
are fickle at best

rub an eye
chew an apple

the wonderful thing
about babysitting
is that you can still smoke pot
and get away with it

the ears are sore
from the teacher pulling them

he was always a fool
always breaking pencils
in front of an audience of one

don't scratch that itch
it will turn crimson
and no scabs will heal it

Please Don't Burn Me

black on
black off

piss in the stomach
sugar on the oak tree

a stone blanket
a garden of oil

jesus hanging from a parachute
balancing butter and jam
on a piece of burnt toast

how it is so beautiful
to see a lighthouse with no fog

how ugly it is
to see a leaf blower blowing leaves

a fan spins
like a whirlpool

a book smites the words
into your mind

What Do They Say?

i saw a picture
of an upside down cow

blades of steel
as cold as an iceberg

bleeding
cursing
bleeding

a pile of dead debt collectors
in front of the front door

breath full of milk
scratching the side
of the head

buongiorno stupid
look at the glass sharks

hair on the chin coarse
gums ache candy from
yesterday's birthday cake

i saw a flying woman
she sang to me
in the sweetest voice

For Seamus

he was adored
in public
in private

he dug out the poems
from the dirt

he toiled in the field
to find the right words

still derry
after all these years

a cottage with a robin's
nest in its thatched roof

he sang
the songs
of people
of both sides

he laughed at bad jokes
spoke seriously about
the troubles

goodbye
you were the best
you were mystical

Stir It, Stir It

mango bat wings
black thumbs
like daggers in the dark

persephone was brash
but too young

shower hot
shower cold

i ask of you
why do you cough?

i thought that the lingering
of milkshake smoke
makes you sweeter
not bitter

veins play on the piano
arrows pierce the fetid air

i am a nut
that belongs
with other nuts

the water of the merced river
is not drinkable

In Order

she wore her pimples
like a polka dot tie

she moved like a butterfly
as if the wind were pushing her around

reasons for living

#1 air quality is good
#2 he loves me
#3 i can smoke anywhere
#4 car has a full tank of gas

ears pierced
just yesterday

the studs are shiny
the lobes relax

hungry hungry
teeth at the ready
stomach waits like an
apartment ready to move in

the pillows are not too soft
not too hard

Taunt Jesus

maniacal sting
bring me the
cigarette voucher

touch the animal
deep inside the moon
taunt jesus

bless your nose
i am sneezing cockroaches
i am eating a frog

head bliss
dash the bastard
you the amiable picture

before the pan rings
i will take a daily antonym
and make it a circle

wrench the fire
and watch it forget
she is a goblin

Champagne Spillage

it's so cold here
my feet feel like bricks

the sound of white noise
so loud
i feel like my head
is in a beehive

my darling woman
don't break the bottle of
champagne

please dance for me
like setting a clock to the
right time

brown bears
pelicans
a murder of crows

my lovely woman
will you make me an omelet?
with ham and onions

put it on a plate that looks like
the face of a guantanamo prisoner

i won't tell
i promise

Is There A Way?

ouch ouch
the fan hits the crap
with a ton of elephant spit

going to be a spatula
paddling grass
imagining recess

if i could i would
devastate the homemakers

please forgive this gibberish
i don't know it either
but the cigarette likes scabs

fool fool fool
the cockroaches won't
beam light into your eyes

it was funny once
when the ice cream man coughed
up little nuggets of crow

yes i am being a dolt
as you can tell my mind
is in the andromeda galaxy

Itchy, Scratchy

gulag jello
bring the heat of
your face to me

i am a transformed
mushroom
a morel

itch in my brain
why does deet
clamor on my skin?

brilliant woman
i cherish your small feet
i cherish your curves
curves that my hands drive on

really bored
that the television
has a hole in it

going to the prostitutes
home in the mountains

for a while
it looked like she would be
a blueberry for the rest
of her life

I Thought That Was Crazy

can monsters enter
the uterus?

wash cycle on
warm as a peacock

she cooked a meal
of stale fish and broken glass

where are the demons?
i hear them
but i can't see them

stoked fire
a tailored suit

go to the nervous
that makes you throw up

go to the eden
where you can have
an apple as food
and a snake for a pet

Women Are Right

the exhaust smells like a skunk

she painted her nails in the shape
of a uterus

power to women all over the world

the congresswoman filibustered
for 10 hours straight

nobody was going to tell them
how to use their bodies

i agreed

i with the hanging appendage
i with the beard
i with the two spheres

they wore orange
it was a good color

and i hoped they won

Try To Be Hopeful

it's finally wednesday
i can take the candy tranquilizer
and have my fun

the ancient speakers
played an imaginary
radio station

them telling him
to die
to die

as bright as a red light
he couldn't think
he couldn't laugh

but sometimes when he
thinks of that evil day
he can breathe in the smog
and still feel calm

that train took him to
the desert
it was 100 degrees that day
nobody cared

Rattling In The Dark

you broke my heart
with a cigarette

clogged clogged
the stones rattle
in your stomach

you sent the demons
to a place called goodbye

you made a pact with
me to make sure i would
love you always

but one thing that stuck
was the tar in the arteries

clenched teeth
you wanted to yell out
and say that this is not
all it's supposed to be

sad face
go away
i want to feel like
a bush on fire

Comfortable Or Solitary?

hornet dusting
the mountains can't speak
snow covers their mouths

river runs
river walks
river stumbles

eyebrow hair
breaks a seed
when does the party start?

why the solitary?
why the last?
why the comfortable?

rings a note
that tells you that
you must recede

like a balding man

Go Cookie Monster!

her tears told the story
octopus library
there is no becoming a saint

forlorn looks into the void
i am a turtle in that race
doily dress is tacky

taste the heart tattoo
pierce your nipple target
soiled underwear in the laundry

wait now
as i cup the coffee into my hands
let the blowfish die first

she never ate cookies
she had nightmares of cookie monster
eating her hands

yawn yawn
bring the heat to the living room
sad face sad face

if it were plausible
i would chew metal
to get rid of this cigarette breath

Drinks Are On Me

my eyes hang on
the edge of a cliff

that's what it feels like
when i'm tired

fat fantasy
a good vodka
drink it ice cold

throat full of cobwebs
i clear it
and a thousand spider babies
crawl in my mouth and nose

this is it
the final goodbye
and you won't know it either

the fingers of a socialite
are glitter pink
are spotted owls

go to the store
and pick out a bored pickle
pick out a loving dead cow

Is It Cold Enough?

weasel nose
ice down the back
crushed peppers inhaled

so the reason why you
are going to tallahassee
is because prison is too kind to you

swallow the aspirin
shake hands with the enemy
little darling you are a plume of smoke

let it burn
let it burn
but drink a glass of water

we have an obligation
to make people better
not worse

we have the right to not
shoot someone
or something

20 years of bickering made
her stomach into torn up
pieces of paper

Weird Is The New Good

a dock full of ants
tired toenails want to be
hammered into the soil

ketchup smile?
no
mustard frown

he backed up the driveway
and barely missed a daisy on
the ground

itchy soul?
no
content pool full of beer

so why did she buy a snake?
maybe she was lonely
too lonely

eyes of saturn
blotches of seaweed

i'm here too
within the maelstrom
coming up for air

That Was Her, Alright

her eyebrows were
perfectly formed

i thought her landing strip
was blonde

it was

the oven bakes a cat
a robin sings the blues
with sweetness

bash your head on the door
hear silence like a cupcake
like a bruise on the arm

break the window with a sword
taunt the toddler with a
bottle of milk on a string

going to atlanta
and i will open a deli

she is the right astronaut
for the drive home

It's Going To Cost You

butterscotch cigarette
i box the kangaroo with a
fistful of brick dust

her lecture was serious
then why did she have a
smile on her face when she
said
get real?

the smiles of a thousand monkeys
tell me that even
though life is hard
you can be happy too

two moons
two fingers on the pulse
two different colored eyes

i am a celebrity
but people lie to me
you want this?
you want that?

it's going to cost you

Yes, It Did Happen

empty the ashtray
burning burning

i brought a dog with me
a springer spaniel

parts and parts
twisted metal
a perpetual fog of smoke

stunned
bring your sorrows
stir the spoon

she was on the phone that day
and then it went silent
for the 11th day was cursed

my fear is to be
in that tin can
and the box cutters work

goodbye my friends
goodbye my family

we will survive

A Million Lullabies

jump into the caramel darkness
bring out a couple of eyes
coated in sugar

a fly stuck in his throat
hands shake
feet quiver

tons of eons of dust
of dirt
of sky

the threat to bring
all the world into the sun
won't happen for millions of years

but it will happen nonetheless
and it will be the brightest fireworks
display in history

beg for the coins
the coins that jingle in
my firm pocket

free the iguana
and let the insects die
that's how it's supposed to be

Where They Are

creases in the sky
i see a planet revolving
around my eyelids

both sides of the neck
are freezing

i will be an ice sculpture
i will be a piece of freezer
burned chicken

lights are on
lights are off

taper the stomach
and disregard the hole
make it solid

guerilla marketing
that's what my mom told me

as long as the car
is running
you should be able to
drive off a cliff

Did That Really Rhyme?

goldfish fall to the ground
kissing all the way down

your front porch was clean
it was there where i got on one knee

three children and 25 years
it's been really good
really good

have i stopped smoking?
have i stopped drinking?
have i stopped snoring?

it will be a good night tonight
because i'll see him

that old fart

before he got old
we would cringe at the loud sounds

before the ice cream melted
he would scream like a hawk

Little Angers

when is it time to go?
he is as red as a drunk sunset

the knives fly out
of his mouth

his grip burned
on your arm

you talked to the luckiest
man in town

before you knew it
he put two martinis down your throat

he brushed your fingers
with little kisses

no wonder he was livid
when you told him he would
never touch your bra straps

he would never see the inside
of your panties

better go now
before he runs you down
with his mercedes-benz

Psychotic Kiss

she gave me a psychotic kiss
on my cheek
may the mark never go away

i saw her one night
pink miniskirt
a sable coat

and those stiletto heels
just the way i like them

i felt sad that i was
in love with a prostitute

we used to balance
her checkbook twice a week

went grocery shopping on
sundays
that was her day off

i thought
how could she let all
those men enter her?

For Ezra

mr. pound
i do not like you
but i like your poetry

you the jew hater
you the old man
you the translator extraordinaire

how i would've liked to
have met you

i would slap you on
your right cheek

and kiss your left

mr. pound
i hope you are satisfied
that your legacy continues
to this very day

gertrude stein was your mother
alice b. toklas was your father
or was it the other way around?

the last thing i would do is
tattoo the numbers 0001 to your hand

Don't Make It Quick

strawberry cacophony
ears of corn listen to
the laughter

mon dieu
sparkling water
a crow caws

broken thumb
will you heal fast?

crooked smile
will you ever
straighten yourself out?

the taste of marlboro reds
on your lips

i won't kiss them
i won't kiss them

you clean the sheets this time
you make the pancakes
you squeeze the oranges

That's Not The Way To End It

weeds weeds weeds

you smoke and
you cough

why do you smoke?

weeds weeds weeds
weeds weeds weeds

i think it is best to shoot
the bullet at the temple

slap a rose
onto her forehead

laugh at the bad
complexion in the mirror

weeds weeds weeds

do you think your heartless
banter will make me insane?

if the wolves howl tonight
then i will rake leaves in the moonlight

Lovely, Lovely

a thousand kisses
a thousand blushes

my smile means that
i won't regret
being with you

you swallow down
a glass of sherry

i smoke a camel
in the darkening day
with rain splashing down

you touch my hand
i feel a thousand needles
piercing it

i touch your cheek
you feel a thousand petals
stroke it

you know
in bed
was like scratching
an itch

II.

Black Eye

hiccup madness
the salt tastes the meat
the meat sticks out its tongue

weasel
open the dining room table
catch a moth
desist

jello pudding
i don't like bill cosby
but that commercial was really funny

books
knives
clocks

i bought a suitcase
full of almonds
salted and smoked

you're a wish away
from getting nothing
but a black eye

Breakage

madness
occult
the beaver rakes

diary
dairy
i dare you to eat

sublet
water
she splashes the
perfume into her eyes

broke
open
he will always make faces

quiz
desk
mr. hotchkiss ran into a student's car
with his new miata

artichoke
dance
something's going to break

It Fell From His Lips

water in the cup
sip it
drink it

poor bobby
he never knew his son
liked needles

there weren't any tests
back then

but when he finally
let the truth fall from his lips

everyone listened

drinking beer
on a saturday night

the television is broken
so the sheets get dirty again

she injured his ribs
but that's alright

tomorrow they will heal
and she will tickle him again

Smashing And Breaking

when the book speaks
you listen

when the clock taunts
that it's time to get up
you curse

when the beetle
shuffles under your foot
you smash

i can't tell if your
eyes are red or black

but i do know that you smoke
camels under a phosphorescent lamp
that catches moths

a broken apple
a split heel

my mom tells me to
not forget the day i ate
an ice cream cone with
that run away dog sabre

What Is Dandruff?

fresh jesus
fresh apples
fresh bananas

i took the anger
and stumped it out
in the ashtray

i took the anger
and flushed it down
the toilet

itchy scalp
what is dandruff?
can a raven sing in white?

wrinkle the blankets
cast out the dirty water
and hold on to the torn pages

save the broken pasta
wring out the tampon
and keep the broken glass at bay

struck by malaria
he would see the devil as jesus
jesus as the devil

Is He Dead Or Alive?

dust transformer
crackle crackle
the sea of galilee is full

lick the lips
scratch the itch
she is beautiful

bring the wet towel
and snap to attention

stir the coffee
and slurp the sugar

my hair is long and straight
butterflies wince when they
see a bee on their flower

radio on
radio off

her almond brown eyes
say i am a good person

as always

The Food Is Alive

bubbles
on the toast

bleeding butter
jam is envious

break the bacon
crisp and greasy

i am not a saint
and neither are you

you bought a dress
so lovely

a sea green

it reminded me of the
air when it feels pure
and fresh

all of my life
all i ask is for someone to
be happy for me

It Happened Revisited

at noon today
they will declare it
kill an arab day

this year
9/11 passed by quickly
and quietly

like december 7th
every year in the distant past

people would throw rocks
into japanese people's windows

we never forget
but we never forgive

hair falling out
i'm getting older and older
but have about 40 years left

crisp apple
please don't bleed on me

crunchy carrot
please restore my eyesight

Mr. Stallone

circles of victims
a murder of crows
near my rain stained window

a cut on the finger
they woke me up
with a click
with a snap

balding
bad breath
a loose tooth

she still enjoys talking
about the day she met
sylvester stallone

soiled underwear
crazy eights
a dog eared page

5 times they made a run
for the border
on the 6th time they either
drowned or the heat got them

Then It Was True

flies flies everywhere!
just choose the right cheese

mountains get in the way
of the transcendence of flying objects

a tick in a man's leg
bloopers on the dinner table

beers beers everywhere?
i want to drink them all
and let my face be a clown

for you i would give you a
kiss on the forearm

don't let the drake
destroy your life

he only wears a corn blue tie
and has his superiors
in his ear

veins burst
tickling a squirrel
and i want ball bearings

A Broken Headboard

wasting away
in this cannibal soup

water balloons
thrown from a car
thrown from an obelisk

two lovers
one bed
a broken headboard

cover the sores
with psychotic kisses

dread the night
when all light goes out
this is purgatory

bags under eyes
streaks of red
a beleaguered girl

tastes the rain

wish for a stomach
that can hold iron and lead

Stop The Madness

cherry tomato
you bring me luck
when the sun disappears

itch on the eye
a tear fears it will not
be welcome on the cheek

lips of steel
you blew the moon away
the stars blinked twice
they are afraid

the stomach asks for forgiveness
as the liver yawns
as the intestines wind away
into the dark

to be an apple that is
as red as a hibiscus
you were wrong about me

life gives the dandelions
a fighting chance

stop the madness from
seeping into the dark
cursing all the way

Immortality

being this close to immortality
will make my ego soar into the
atmosphere like an airplane

conjure the muffin
break the book
into little tiny spaces

itchy armpits
she is a limpid pool
full of grease

i am not who i think i am
forget the snot
forget the ear wax

please take the garbage
and burn it to the ground
or else i will fail at math

toxic breath
the robins wander to
the pond and an alligator
eats them

easy to easy
save the life
of an indigent disc

White Hair Worn Short

blues blacks
a cardinal lands on the
table and cannibalizes
the turkey breast

her white hair worn short
tickle of sugar on the tongue
why the saddest face of all?

blue and red strings on the
backs of my hands

shaking
having a good time
until the beer runs out

a slipped disc
a broken collar bone
a sprained knee

she carried a bucket of oil
to the hut
and lit it on fire to ward
off the malaria

The Day Time Stopped

skittles flew everywhere
the soda spilled on the ground

blood and soda
mixed together
making a kind of flammable liquid

broken gun
why did you work
this one time?

why didn't you listen?
they told you no
but you followed anyway

now you wear your suit
and alligator tears are in
your blank brown eyes

the jury said no
and this time you agreed

what the hell
is wrong with you?

child killer
murderer of a thousand slaves

Skin A Cow

i hate to say
this but you are
a demon in disguise

play the flute with
gnarled gin

fingers aorta
glutton of fun

it's not the temper
it's the diaper full
of toys and dolls

i am a brigand
stealing the sword
that goes into your mouth

i am the asteroid bastard
that takes a whip
and skins a cow

forlorn memories
i forget the fickle
i remember the savage

Domestic Violence

finish beating the eggs already
you beat them more than
you beat me last night with
a baseball bat!

cook them on high
go ahead and burn them
just like when you put out
your cigars on my skin

add some ham
add some onions
it will cry just like i cried
when you slapped me on the cheek

turn it over
yes turn it!
just like you turned me over
and fucked me silly

slide it out of the pan
put it on a plate
you won't break teeth
but i did when you punched me

Scratch

these black half moons
under my eyes
i don't know what sleep is

the burnt yellow on my middle finger
the tattoo of cigarettes
my breath a cherry mess

pressure pressure
i know of steel bands
i know of hand slapped against cheek

rub the chicken
scratch that lottery ticket
read the poems

and how those words
will hurt like a hangnail

not bloody
but throbbing

not angry
but crimson

i don't have the energy
to argue

We Don't Have To Suffer

burning calves
ache in the goat
i was a lollipop
that was being sucked

if the moms
of the world eradicate
the midnight disease

then all would be well

a shout here
a scream there

the stomach wreaks havoc
on the pizza

he sleeps on the couch
and dreams of a lifetime
of not suffering

but won't we all be the same
if we didn't suffer?

remember
that the truth is not the
only solution

Bladder Control Not A Problem

heart jumps
like a salmon working
its way upstream

god wants to
flood the world again

i understand now
she bangs her head
against the wall

blueberries
cheers!

granny smith apples
thank you!

coughing was not
on the agenda

please please
take this ring off my finger

bladder control
not a problem

Never Forget

bastard son
of nazis

the cream colored ashes
caught in his blue eyes

distant relatives
wanted him to live
with them

but he refused
the iron cross stuck
to his heart

sauerkraut
bratwurst
oktoberfest

lies
the lies
that men and women tell

he was just a forgotten memory
he was a dull coin in the
wash basin

Maid's Daily Work

awesome
awesome

sue was a trained potty cleaner

drown the feces
get rid of the urine

wash your hands of
the deep sugar of the night

her tongue was as dry as
an iguana's skin

her face as beautiful as
the queen of hearts

say this
out loud
i am a smart person

nobody will believe you

I Thought It Was Okay

play that movie
wash the clothes
the sky is purple today

play the record
wash the windows
the air is hot today

scared of clouds?
pull out hair
and paint the eyes pink

dirty fingernails
black soles
a penguin is eating a piece of clam

swallow the ice cream
wipe the drained mouth
i am a wicked king playing executioner

she was a long legged shiny
she was a blank face of woe
she was a lucky power ball guesser

my beard itches
there is asphalt in it

What's Fracking?

a fracking yard
never heard of it
until now

leprechaun blood
on the bully's shoes
he didn't get the gold though

2 am
it is too early to go
to bed

but my eyes say otherwise

a knot in my stomach
i sailed the seas of rocks and clams
rotten meat
not good

tongue touches hers
my lips have a seizure

dolled up and ready to go
her place between betty white
and patrick stewart

The Sharks Come

roses in my cheeks
bananas in my teeth

sharks circle around my heart
waiting for the right time to
strike again

i feel that a thousand things
are a cherished picture

i took your picture with
my eyes

i will not forget
i will not forget

through the glass house
i find a slipper
that belonged to you

in the closet
i saw you there
kissing my teddy bear

i miss your sweet scent
in the failing light

i miss your happy breasts
the ones i always liked the best

Does It Rhyme? Part 2

beat the old couch
into submission

make kisses with
the fishes

if i could
i would make brie cheese illegal

don't forget the pepper
it makes the food taste better

shaking the chicken
he baked it and made a
mess of it

brown sugar
own the spatula
crown the steak

allen you dastardly poet
i know you want to eat
and eat a lot

Blush At The Thought

a sprig of cherry blossom
slept through spring
and bit summer on the cheek

a nameless scab
on the hand
will talk shit about you

smoke a joint
and make it feel like
a hammer beating on the head

someone said no
because they were not truthful
to the sun and moon

trust the love that was a present
to you on your birthday

it will always keep you warm
it will always keep you company

dance for me
while the peacock filters by

sing for me
while the songs of birds
keep me smiling

Falling Falling

gallbladder blandness
she was smarter than a dictionary
catch the baseball with bare hands

i do
i do
i do

what idiot wouldn't?

the river is swollen
the apple trees in full bloom

down the road
there is a house
full of butterflies

dear sister
did i make sure i protected you?

teeth are going to fall
out someday
and she'll still love me

A Copy Of My Grandfather

on the death of my grandfather
i'll say only this

the greatest joy was
waking up to the smell of
eggs and potatoes

on a warm summer day
on sunday

he would get the dog
to bark at my grandmother
time to eat!

swimming
walking
eating

we did all this under the
disguise of a life well lived

if i could tell my grandfather
one last thing

it would be that i love you
and you were the man i always
wanted to be

What Color?

blue eye
green eye
brown eye

i see you in the thick
of the smog in your heart

a half smile
a toothy grin
a full on brightness
comes to me

like coming up to the
surface after holding my breath
for a couple minutes

next to me
you didn't give up

next to you
i held on and on and on

when the life ends
it will be a flicker

but when we consummate
it will be a fireball in the sky

I'm Not So Sure

this love
like a 105 degree fever
even ice cannot
help it

i see a woman who
can speak
but chooses not to

i feel the hands
that will hold our son
for the first time

it's the first day of autumn
i am dissolving
in your cool glass of water

the leaves dance on the breeze
attachment is such a hard thing to do

i see your perfect feet
trod on the ground soldiers did
many centuries ago

and so i believe
in a sadness that will go away
when you put your hand
on my chest

It Is Real And Surreal

kafka coughed
and all the cockroaches
paused for a moment

i licked my worn lips
they're like hard dirt
they're like broken glass

so tell me maestro
what do you do for a living?

you break backs?
wow i do that too

well not really
i break pencils
i break teeth by chewing
on pens

i tasted ink once
the red kind
i was so sure it would
taste like blood

but it tasted like apple vinegar
on steroids

III.

When The Day Died

i believe the wrecked
towers of steel did not fall
like feathers in the still air

i believe that when the body
jumps into the smoky air
it thinks it will fly

sirens
coughing
screams

those names
haunt me to this day

when the syrup of bravery
pumped in the veins of those
men and women

nobody could understand
how fear was a dissipating fog
in their minds

those tainted terrorists
were blind to mohammed
and they paid for it with death

the torn flag still flies
in the wind of hope
the survival of the soul
must be preserved

Choke And Spit

sweet nipple
why is it that you
always give me
bitter milk?

that diamond necklace
look
it wants to choke you

i will vomit on your
business suit

i will castigate
the sisters and brothers
that i don't have

popcorn kernels
stuck in my throat

a pea up the nose

a bean in my ear

i will never leave
i will be the one who will
bury you both
when you die

Ghost Town

i'm as cold as a freezer
in a refrigerator

she pierced the left ear
it felt like an injection
searing searing

he walked the streets
of his hometown
and found out that it was
actually a ghost town

play the music
of the angels

listen to the ice cream
sliding down the throat

i smell lime
in the beer

i touch the red and brown leaves
summer has left us
like a petty mistress in a
dress that touches her toes

National Hero

so sad
that her visit has ended

i stare at the uneaten
french fries

there's a cool breeze

they are still here
being crazy
driving me crazy

i'll soon find the spot
on the couch
which is mine

its playoff time
the man that steroids built
a national hero

she tugs on her gown
we didn't wear it this high
she mumbles

the clock ticks
my bladder is full

and she gives me my meds

Things Are Just Things

the setting of forks and spoons
seems like a meaningless task
unless you like to eat with your hands

picking up the children at school
may seem trivial
until someone kidnaps them

a ring on a pinkie
where the boats go at night
nobody knows

if a weed could talk
it would plead to you not
to pull it out of the ground

if a bookshelf could eat
it would eat only poetry books

uneven eyebrows
unruly beard

the temps are rising
and god laughs
because he wants you to know
what hell feels like

Calibrate The Distance

concrete ice cream
coconut braces

thumbs all blue
because the piano
is broken

temps in hell
tattoos grasp onto
stiff flesh

pull that muscle
break that ankle
strain that knee

forgotten rubies
in her teeth
i saw dorothy there

calibrate the distance
from her face
to yours

and then there will be
a storm from the north
that will break everything

Time In Merced

cough drop cigarette
why do you make my
eyes itch?

what did they
do to you?

so i looked at the woman
with large breasts

so i watched a dog
pee on a tree

stomach acid
burps
a fluffy pancake

now look what you did!
they are watering
they are freezing in the
zero degree temperature

call me
and tell me
merced is waiting for me

Torturer Or Torturee?

cashew brain
lullaby heat
on a bunch of hot coals

realize that the horses
have ping pong balls
in their nostrils

go in between the
crazy and sane

break a stone
on your grindstone nose

where the swallows go
when they arrive in the dusk
nobody knows

i'm a really great pretender
she's a really great faker

half smile
maybe a grin

dust settles in the eyes
red red red

Season Of Giving

my head hurts
from the constant
ball being bounced
inside my skull

is it summer yet?
there are snowflakes here
winding down to the
grey worn grass

didn't know that he was
a mailman
until he pulled out a bottle
and drank from it

i could smell the whiskey
on his breath

The Tooth Doctor

lice in the hair
worms in the stomach
dye in the eye

sabotage the golden gate
don't jump
don't jump

on my way
to the tooth doctor
i hate the stains
i hate the chips

ice on a platter
heart of a lion
still looked for

dust off the mirror
it can tell you anything
except what you are thinking

crunchy fingers
screech why?

dancing puddles
in the middle of the dark

Rabbit's Hole

behind me
the volcano climaxed

it was red hot
and i couldn't touch it

in front of me
my beating heart
drank my blood

i couldn't stop it
she took my check

as the mountain rises
in the east

as the ocean sets in
the west

i capture the cold
that makes it harder
to breathe smog

click click
down the rabbit's hole

Pretty Ugly

he grew his beard
until it touched the ground

periwinkle in his hair
a loose fitting tie around his neck

perfume perfume
smell the sweetness
and bury your nose into her hair

she smiles
as if the world has ended
and she was the last pregnant
woman on earth

don't rot
don't simmer
don't bake

attention trees
we are going to cut you down
and the leaves agree

bees congregate
and their pollen filled bellies
are going to make honey someday

Ouch Is The Word I'm Thinking Of

got out of the car
she jammed my heart
in the door

i yelped
like an injured dog
blood pooled on the concrete

i guess she doesn't
love me anymore

i asked her if she could
open the door and release
my heart

with ice on her cheeks
she silently opened the door

i cleared my throat
no lips are going to
touch mine tonight

i just couldn't say it
the word wouldn't come out
but goodbye flashed in my mind

Select All

vanilla ice cream
on my moustache
hell would be worse
dog crap flavor

hair falling out
bald spot on the sun
mercury tries to make love
to venus

but they can't seem to meet
at the right place

kraken
oh kraken
take me away

into your deep depths
or eat me
i don't care
as long as you cease the pain

hole in the tooth
hole in the roof
the nails spill on the ground
like grey icicles in winter

Bukowski Was Here

the sun
that blatant sun
where is the cool wind
when you need it?

the moon
that demure moon
when the stars come out
we know that it is time to kiss

shadows come
shadows go

and i know that this is
a time when i am able
to love once again

the smoke comes from
a statue that is
holding a cigar

the break between wind and
silence
comes sooner than expected

College Days

freshman year in college
was my best year academically

but the women
swimming in and out
of my bed

made the homework
hard to accomplish

the cheerleader girl
the one with the glass eye
she was cute
too cute

an alarm went off in my heart
this is right
this is wrong

she shaved me
and when she nicked my chin
i didn't even feel it

she made dinner every time
she came over
oh that chicken cacciatore was delicious

Interesting Facts

rummaging and cathartic
blueberries iced in the freezer

fond of the phrase
don't forget

is better than the phrase
you're bad

algae clings to the roof
of your mouth

your painted on eyebrows
are bleeding

a lump in the stomach
is she pregnant again?

i can see the planet venus
in the sky

it looks like someone took a thumb
tack and poked a hole in the dark

Broken And Blunt

headache city
count the burps
coming out of your mouth

blue hues
incontinent disease

solid teeth
the theme is the same
as the other ones

he is arriving at noon
with a bottle of whiskey
with a single suitcase

blunt blunt
the broken bones
have a say in this

darling darkness
being a leper
bring me peace

sovereign lover
to be is to not like
a single malt scotch

For Lori Williams

i'm going to miss you
my friend of a few moons

you liked tom
and you rubbed it in
everyone's faces

you liked naked people
in the subway
on the streets

the good ones
are always taken early

why is that?
i wonder

no more pain
no more tears
no more frowns

i see you smiling
next to your mom and dad

She Wasn't Fat, Just Husky

sliding glass cigarette
your smoke mocks me

as i inhale
as i exhale

nicotine stains
my lungs

a freight train
ashes for tracks

earring
nose ring
a pierced eyebrow

the glowing light fades
and i am alone with
the cockroaches

around my feet

steady now
the boat won't sink

as long as you keep
the orange peels near
your nose

numbers and letters
i hate the symbol &
in anything written

madness has taken the rabbit
down the nasty smelling hole
she will birth a yellow baby made
of gold

Mirror, Mirror

she said
you are not ugly
you are beautiful

as the mirror stared back

she said
you smell like lilacs

as her nose sniffed the air

she said
you are a dress that
fits perfectly

as her body twisted and turned

she said
you have a good heart

as the beating in her chest
hurts her very much

she said
leave me at the moon's doorstep
and i will love forever

as the man who walked into her life
shuts the door behind him

Reach For The Vodka

breaking bricks on my head
this headache will not go away

peace comes to me when
i finally reach for the vodka

heart skips every so often
i am not a metronome
i am not a ticking clock

my nose itches
i scratch it
it turns red as a turnip

my throat is clogged
with nicotine phlegm
and i can't breathe

busted toe
i can't walk
it hurts
it hurts

taste the smoke
of the incinerator

realize that this life
is only an illusion

For Jeannine

sweat forms on her
arms

she looks like a villainess
with an agenda

to destroy men

dirt kicked up
boots are not shiny anymore

she tugs at her left ear
as the fire keeps on burning

the invisible cat
scurries across the road

you can see it when it eats
the shiny sharp teeth snapping
and crunching

she punched a hole through
the car window

and choked the vagrant to death

Thanks A Lot

were you that lonely
that you had to fall into her
and prick the dried apricot?

i'm ashamed of you
i thought you were the pope
i thought you were the president

now i know that
you will betray at every end
taking lives and have
everyone in your life suffer

black rocks
grey rocks
rocks with sharp points

they should be hurled at you
and the end is whatever happens

i will smoke my pipe
and wait for the ambulance
they will know what to
do with you

you were never my friend
you were never my lover

DMV And Gorillas

oh so tired
oh so achy

when the pain stops
i'll know i'm a dead leaf

retake the test
mark circle c
over and over

passed

with

flying colors

what hurts the most
is the gorilla on my back
the one choking me

from behind

shiny
made of titanium
these dentures are solid

Burning, Burning

the devastation of the days
makes the sun drip tears of sorrow

burning
burning

a half smile
does she know it now?
it has been so long

i'm not down
i'm not up
nothing left to lose

in her hands
she has seeds
grow
let them grow!

break down the walls
walk right on through
and i'll be on the other side
waiting for you

then sleep
sweet sleep
to take us away
to our desert island

What Does This Mean?

oh when we were washed up
the women stall on the take off
and crash to the ground

friends come and go
but family always stays
in your ears

as the words were clear
it was a ghost telling me
that the world was going to end

sing out loud
someone will hear you
and they will smile

when the right closes
and the left one stays open
are you a pirate?

garbage collects on the floor
spiders bite caught flies
and an ice cream truck brings

the end of an
era of being a child

When It All Comes Together

charmed by a stink bug
the dung beetle is his father
the cockroach his mother

bricks stacked high to
the brilliant blue skies
i turn to ash

combination
of hotdogs and hamburgers
mustard and ketchup
envious of each other

bingo bingo
the tail light fails
she bought a conch shell

find the tight way
find the right way
find the splendid time

miss the rock
on the road
but hit the deer
while picking up your
dropped burrito

Jamming

touch the apple on the
top of its stem

you will gain a friend
you will gain a lover

don't slurp your noodles
only japanese people do that

and you aren't japanese

he parked his car on the street
turned on the alarm
not that it would work

strode into the diner
ordered a coffee black

she came a few minutes later
no soap
but clean nonetheless

she showed him the outline of
her bra
when nobody was looking

Denied

that's enough
you broke her panties
and she was slobbering
all over the pillow

she curled up into
a little ball
and denied you entrance

you burned your tie
you poured gasoline onto it

you stuck out your tongue
and bit it off

you looked into the mirror
and cut off your nose

slowly slowly
you fall asleep in
your own blood

she will wake up the next morning
and scream into the early light

i should have she sobs
i should have

Differing Opinions

intense love
the shock of it
made humans drown

crack crack
watermelon seeds
a parakeet imprisoned

she brought a key
lime pie

it was tasty
and smooth

right right
the beginning of a relationship
the end of a friendship

shave the legs
twitch the eyebrow
cast the last stone into
the cockroach carcass

Bruce

i'm sorry
but we are all out of
patience here

i'm going to have sex
with my neighbor's wife

make a salsa dip
and bring the tortilla chips

the cough is persistent
but mighty joe will suppress it

bruce lee
was the master
he played ping pong with a
pair of nun chucks

fingers raw and cold
the shrimp would swim away
if they could get out of the net

no cuts
no bruises
no broken bones

Never Faithful

she liked naked apartments
she liked broken fences
with the moon painted on them

flashback
to the time when
all you had to worry about

braces
pimples
wearing the cool clothes

she was the one who
looked like a chameleon
always moving from
boyfriend to boyfriend

never lasted because
all she wanted was sex
and when she got it
that was it

i remember murdering my heart
over her

i wanted to show her someone who
could love her and stay

It Was Always Wet

irregular bowel movements
a lion chases a gazelle

bloody pulp
the pink rose
blooms in the morning sun

really?
i thought it was a lie

nose plugged with mucus
a smile came from the baby
after he ate

changing the sheets
wet sex
wet towels on the bed

crash in west hollywood
that party must have been good

hot chocolate
mixed with toothpaste
an awful combination

cigars burn in the ashtray
a full stomach
a woodpecker pecks at the wood

IV.

Hot Hot Hot

the tropics are hell
and i'm not exaggerating either

first you fry bacon on the
back of your neck

boil the coffee on your cheeks

the sweat feels like an oil slick
that has been broken

broken
yes the heat breaks you
into scrambled eggs
and butter

scabs become scars
scars become war heroes

war heroes become absent
of thought and in the final
conclusion it's better to have a band aid

madness
yes that too
like flies buzzing in your head

Pain Is Pain

there's a cage around my heart
you put it there

took the key
and swallowed it
i'm not going anywhere soon

you brought a tray of mangoes
and bread

a cup of water
with ice in it

you still treated me
like a stranger
in your house

even when i sat on the couch
you lingered near the kitchen

but i saw you looking at my lips
by then they were warm and red

did you want to kiss me?
did you want to hold me?

i doubt my own decisions
and now i will fade into black

Drunk Bastard

buckle the belt
don't lash at him
this time

let the beer enter
your dirty mouth

let the beer enter
the seas of cheese and
acid

the television is on
but there is nothing on

isn't that what they say
at 3 am?

another beer
is opened

it sounds like
a cracked knuckle

jam and jerry
would the playing of
the piano be

too repetitive?

Bad Stuff

the teeth in her mouth
look like a labyrinth

he bothers me like
a fly trying to get
into my mouth

a bathing suit
is a toothpick

a table is a cold blue
when the meals get served
aphrodisiacs rejoice

i am not sane
i am not insane

i do not feel
i am not a sociopath

cough the limericks
drop the jaw into the sink

out of the blur
there is a person who
was born for wrinkles

Gentle And Hard

he had stones for eyes
the grey round ones

he knew if he looked at a woman
they would not be able
to see who he was

his hands were made of dandelions
how the children wanted to
blow the seeds into the wind

tongue burnt
teeth rotten
dragon breath

he doesn't know how to talk
to the people he loves most
he slaps them with insults

if the sun were as alive as the heart
then you would know what burns
inside of his chest

i wonder if i could tell him
it's okay
it's okay

Is Love Really This Difficult?

its beyond my control
the way i feel about you

i thought for the longest time
that i would be a hermit
without wings

i thought i was going to
be a camel so thirsty to drink

but then i realized
that i'm not alone
i'm not alone

get rich
and make someone happy

get thin
and make a balloon drift
on top of the limpid lake

when i say yes
i mean it

do you?

When I Was Broken

there is free space in my mind
now i will fill it with her thoughts
and ideas

she wore a low cut blouse
blue and frilly

i took my crutches
and put them beside the table

we drank water and coffee
had a slice of apple fritter
we shared

her paintings were delicious
i could piss on them
and they would still be perfect

i'm not going to watch
television anymore

i'm not going to break
a bone anymore

i lied
i want to dance
i want to skateboard

Angel On Prozac

i am a madman in disguise

behind this gentle
and calm facade
is an angel on prozac

dirty hair
rash on the leg
i'm the victim

she woke me up early
smack my bitch up day

but i'm not violent
just confused

i love her
but i don't know
if she'll love me back

stepping stone?
genuine?
fake?

make sure you save some money
for food

Oh The Pains!

i first felt it in my back
then my legs
and finally my toes

when my heart was exposed
to the snow
it ran bloody
all the way into the gutter

she bought a piece of carrot cake
and took little bites out of it
when she walked down the street

i felt those bites
mosquitos
surrounding my body

she found a vendor
and bought a cup of hot coffee
she sipped it slowly as
the sun started to rise

i felt those sips
like a vacuum in my veins

i won't remember the words
she whispered when she was
finally home

but i will see the diamonds in
her eyes

It's Pretty Bad

urn full of feces
the underdark is going
to eat you dead or alive

hot today
but the ice cream doesn't melt

cold tomorrow
he is a face full of contradictions

why did i break the awning?
goodbye weasels of anarchy

salacious woman
your buddhist mind
is a timid mouse

please make the scary people
go away

please make the devil
eat his own tail

should there be a talisman of sports?
should there be a cautious bible?

Message In A Bottle

when everything is torn
breaking waves on the sore
wet sand

she walked along the beach
and found a bottle with
a message in it

she took out the piece of paper
and read it

it said
if you fall in love with me
please return me to the sea

she cried for a moment
knowing how empty that
bottle was without the piece of paper

she returned the bottle to the sea
and she waved it goodbye

she let the moment pass
and the moment was as quiet and
as peaceful as it had been
for a very long time

Black Or Strawberry?

tongue soup
that's what they called it
in that foreign land

stitch the pants
caress the teeth
make bullets from
rotten books

sounds of led zeppelin
are caught on an apple tree

was the cockroach black
or was it strawberry?
i don't want to know what
they smell like

daily he rinsed his feet
in duck blood

daily he boiled oil
and added ass sweat to it

wonder why the earth is round?

This Math Doesn't Work

add and subtract
divide and multiply

drive the car off the cliff
and remember the broken elevator

his bony nose
makes me want to
cut it off

her breasts
the ones i loved the most
were cut off

feeling a little giddy today
she was a cool customer
on a very hot day

scratch itch
bake cook
swap the oven for the frying pan

eyebrow senator
please don't vote i don't know

nobody will believe you
nobody will trust you

Woman Crazy

that girl
she drives me off
the cliff
without a parachute

that girl
she makes my skin break out
on the hottest days

i clasped my hands
and said a prayer

no more pain
no more pain
please

i took a piece of paper
and put a pen into my hand

what i wrote i will
not tell you here

but all i will say is that
someone will be happy
getting all my things

It's Broken Again

i'm sorry
but you have taken
everything i ever had

when my heart broke into
a thousand pieces of ice
you let them melt

sigh
a head full of wasps

even the cocaine
didn't work this time

my legs wobble
like a dying spinning top

i look at you and all
i see is a black blanket
hanging over your body

mosquitos bite
the fever rises on my cheeks

but you've already paid
for the coffin

From Big To Massive

goofball airplane
stop doing loops in the
humid air

remember your brother?
he fell from the sky
and burned into ashes

she talked through the
microphone

she was wearing a black
turtleneck sweater

her breasts were massive

the eyebrow hairs
fall to the ground

the fan whirls until
it gets cooler

the weekend is coming
and there will be much beer drunk
mostly cheap 12 dollars for 12 cans

I Saw Your Nipple

some matches
light my mind on fire

damn it
the circles
make it harder to focus

video brain
dance and record
dance and record

shake the cherry stems
from your nipples

cause a riot in
a hospital

being closed
is better than being open

legalize it
people will be responsible
even in the dark

i thought that was awesome
you being the same as me

in the mirror
in the mirror

Float, Relieve, Glide

tired?
take a tylenol pm
and float

float

finished?
clean up
and drift

drift

itchy?
scratch it
and relieve

relieve

cautious?
look both ways
and glide

glide

You Are Not Who You Seem

the ache of
a thousand elephant
trunks hitting the ground

cringing at the brakes screeching
he says don't judge me

you drank too much
you arrogant bastard

sleep with him
and him
and him

heart attack on the waterfront
clam chowder
flows through his veins

lose weight
pull some teeth
clip your toenails

the truth
he says
is not in attention
but flirting

For Tiffany

were the days longer
when we slept in that
summer of '93?

i heard the drunks sleeping
it off in the alley

i heard the groan of the
cat as he stretched and woke up

dirt under the fingernails
only you could get it out
with your trusty knife

rain in the red balloons
lips of caring
a symphony playing in my heart

and you were the soloist
that i had always wanted to hear

It's Not Nice To Frown

takes all night
for the bitter taste in
my mouth to go away

polka dots on her face
lips in a perpetual frown

all i can do is hold
your hand

all i can do is change
your mind

cherries sweet
cherries sour

i rub my cheeks
and take in the chaos

i forget what it's like to
be a man

destitute salacious
but not abusive

Freezing

winter is here now
just like an ex-lover
in your bed one more time

the air feels like
bites from a flea

the sun is not visible
as the clouds cover it
with their lonely blanket

i sit on the porch
wondering when the
rain will finally come

when it does
i will be watching the drops
fall like a bee longs for pollen

my throat is dry
my face is dry

the dogs have gone away
the only animal i see is
the kitten without its mother

They Are Losers

the crackle of my arms
reaching for the itch on my back
makes me miserable

well it does

sneezing and not wiping
my nose disgusts me

well it does

banging on the wall
graffiti on the wall

why does the clock
always read noon?

i am an icon

she is culture

they are losers

and the bone falls to the ground
full of spit
full of headaches

And It Is Finished

so how does hungry sound?
like a lion in the stomach
like a cat hissing

my long neck
looks like a beer bottle

my face
a jigsaw puzzle

when the clock strikes four
the whole world stops
for everything
for nothing

ruined knees
how they said i would
miss you

they were right
when they said
tobacco kills

whirlwind mind
stops on 45
the ball bouncing and bouncing

Steve Baba is a poet and writer from California. He has published 8 poetry collections. Steve grew up in San Jose, California and eventually left his hometown to live in London, England, New York City, Santa Fe, New Mexico and Hawaii. He currently is working on his memoir when he lived in London. An avid reader and cafe patron, Steve lives in San Francisco.

www.ingramcontent.com/pod-product-compliance
Lightning Source LLC
Chambersburg PA
CBHW061727020426
42331CB00006B/1138